LATEST AND GREATEST

TIPSY Scoop™ LLC

LIQUOR-INFUSED ICE CREAM

MELISSA TAVSS AND RACHEL CHITWOOD

The Inside Scoop

STOP RIGHT THERE!

Are you 21?

Security Kyle, Summer 2019

WE ARE GOING TO NEED TO SEE A VALID ID
BEFORE THE BOOZY ICE CREAM MAKING BEGINS...

INTRODUCTION

A Family Tradition:

Tipsy Scoop all started with a family tradition. Once upon a time (like a long, long time ago - in the 1800s!), my Italian ancestors brought ice cream to Scotland. First up was my great, great, great grandfather, Achille, who moved from his small mountaintop town of Picinisco, Italy to Glasgow, Scotland. He made ice cream at home and sold it from a pushcart as he walked the city streets. (Fun fact: Italian men selling food from hand carts came to be called 'hokey pokey' men!) Eventually, he opened his own ice cream shop and brought his sons into the business.

The family business continued with my great, great grandfather, Giovanni, who opened several of his own ice cream shops around Glasgow in the 1900s. My great grandfather, Federico, continuing the tradition, opened ice cream shops throughout Scotland and England and eventually became the President of the Ice Cream Alliance of Great Britain. (Yes - that is a real thing!) A few generations skipped out on the ice cream making tradition...

We had some doctors and lawyers - really nothing very delicious - until finally I brought it back to ICE CREAM in 2014! And with a modern boozy twist!

I started working on my own homemade ice cream recipe (not boozy yet) as soon as my Mom trusted me alone in the kitchen (which was probably not until I was 21 anyway). I found it nearly impossible to get the recipe right in a small Cuisinart ice cream maker. Seriously, how does anyone make good ice cream in those things?!? I was struggling with the consistency - it was coming out all icy on the sides - and decided to add a little tablespoon of alcohol to my ice cream to soften the texture. The alcohol seemed to help, but I wasn't completely happy with my ice cream recipes yet.

At the same time, I was working at an agency doing marketing for different wine and spirits clients. Spending day in and day out exploring tasting notes for different liquors, I had begun to develop a good appreciation for the complexity of flavors that different alcohols brought forward.

Pint Samples, Winter 2013

This was pretty revolutionary to me - that liquors could have complex and interesting flavors; my tastes had really adapted from my college drinking days (cheap and in a plastic handle were my only requirements then). I was certainly very proud of myself for coming to this realization. I began to think - I need more than a tablespoon of alcohol in this ice cream! Why aren't ice cream flavors geared towards more complex adult tastes? Why isn't actually boozy ice cream a thing? We know - there was 'rum raisin' - but come on! That wasn't going to do the trick! I wanted some of those rich flavors I was getting from the alcohol to actually come through in the ice cream!

I started TRYING to learn a little bit more about food science…but it turns out I am not very scientific. So I enlisted the help of a recipe developer. I knew I wanted my ice cream not only to have the flavor of some of the cocktails I loved, but also wanted the ice cream to actually hold an alcohol content! From what I was able to gather from my food science studies, I understood that in a baked treat like a rum cake, the alcohol would burn off when it went in the oven. In ice cream, however, the alcohol wouldn't evaporate but would actually be churned into the ice cream recipe. This meant an opportunity for a food that could actually hold an alcohol content!

BUT - you say - alcohol doesn't freeze, right? Remember the ultimate science experiment - putting a bottle of vodka in the freezer and being shocked that it stays a liquid?!? Yes, we are aware that alcohol does not freeze - but we're not exactly freezing it. We're churning it into the ice cream and infusing it so that the ice cream still holds a soft gelato-like consistency. That being said, our ice cream is on the softer end and more similar to a gelato in texture while still categorized as a hard ice cream.

Now for the fun part (HA)! There's a reason more people haven't implemented this idea to start a boozy ice cream company - it's kind of illegal! Alcohol infused ice cream laws vary state by state. We would go into more detail but fear we are already boring you! Lucky for us, in New York, our liquor-infused ice cream is considered a food as long as it contains less than 5% ABV (which works for our recipes anyway)! We are however, required to provide government warnings, proper labeling, and to card end consumers who purchase our ice cream.

We also got certification as a non-beverage by the Federal government, which means we had to submit all of our recipes flavor by flavor for approval. SO ya...the legal issues and loopholes were not too much fun. We've experienced lots of obstacles along the way, but have a lot of passion behind our idea and our brand and continue to work hard to share it with you!

With the help and feedback from family, friends, and food scientists, I finally perfected the recipes and came up with some creamy, tipsy and delicious treats! And now, following the family tradition, Tipsy Scoop™ is born!

So this is an actual business...

Tipsy Scoop started from an idea - not with a traditional business plan at all. Actually, Tipsy Scoop started in tupperware and mason jars - lots of various containers trying out different flavors that I was constantly sharing with family and friends to get their feedback.

After perfecting the recipe, what came next? With a background in marketing and event planning for different liquor brands, it came naturally to me to pitch my idea to my old clients - what could be more perfect than a boozy ice cream station at the launch of a liquor brand featuring ice cream infused with the liquor brand itself? The idea really gained some traction and before you know it, it was way more than old liquor clients I was catering for. It became friends' weddings - then friends' friends weddings - and before we knew it, we actually developed our own list of clients! As the catering side of the business picked up steam, I decided that it was time to bring someone in to help - my first employee! I called up my old friend Lyz Levy (who I worked with in the liquor marketing biz) and asked her if she was interested in joining the team which at that point was just me! With Lyz's help we moved on to bigger and better things - we added a wholesale component to the business and took our feet to the streets approaching stores all over the city with samples of our boozy ice cream pints. We did everything from pitch the product, make the product, and hand deliver the product to stores! It was quite the labor of love.

Melissa pushing in the cart in NYC, Summer 2015

As our wholesale and catering business picked up, so did our website sales - which was surprising because our website was in horrible shape (like I would definitely be scared to order anything from it). But people did! From there, I brought in Rachel Chitwood, who I met as she worked as a buyer at one of the stores Tipsy Scoop sold to wholesale. I brought Rachel on to help with our website orders and also our nationwide shipping. This was becoming a whole beast in itself - shipping to our wholesalers and delivering direct-to-consumer online orders is a huge part of our business.

At this point, in 2016, I was happy with slowly growing our business as we grew our wholesale and catering accounts and our online/shipping business. At the same time, our Instagram and Facebook followings had been growing rapidly as people started learning about our business. When that happened, we got approached by a few food content companies who wanted to come in and create videos about our company and what we were all about.

In Fall of 2016, these videos were released on Facebook and the response was tremendous. It was a real domino effect. The videos came out one day after the other, and each ended up going viral (with over 7 million views in just 3 days). Our email inquiries, order forms, wholesale and catering sales were completely flooded.

The most surprising effect was that people were showing up at our production facility in East Harlem looking for a boozy ice cream shop (that they saw - or thought they saw - online) and were showing up ready to buy some ice cream.

Opening a brick-and-mortar ice cream shop was never in the business plan, but with the demand clear, I built up the confidence to take the next step and go for it. In May of 2017, we opened our first boozy ice cream Barlour in Manhattan. The response was overwhelming - we had lines OUT the door (and continue to)!

Holiday media preview at the Williamsburg Barlour, Fall 2019

Our neighbors were not fans of all the street traffic we caused but eventually they warmed up to us! In May 2019 we opened our second Barlour in Williamsburg, Brooklyn where we serve boozy ice cream AND ice cream cocktails too. This year we also opened smaller shops in Myrtle Beach, Dallas, and Las Vegas within ITSugar's candy stores. We also offer our ice creams for nationwide shipping via Goldbelly.com and continue to sell wholesale and for catering and events!

Sharing our recipes with you!

For quite a while we were keeping our recipes a secret - but now the secret is out, and we want to share it all with you! We have some amazing flavors that truly have a cult following and wanted to offer YOU the guidance and instruction you need to make boozy ice cream yourself at home. Making boozy ice cream is hard - but making ice cream in general at home is also hard!

We want to help our consumers learn how to tackle this feat – we know you can do it! We have provided recipes for our fan favorite flavors (categorized by the liquor used) and boozy ice cream treats beyond the scoop! We hope to also give you all the info you need to come up with your own boozy ice cream creations. We cannot wait to see what you come up with, so please SHARE!

@tipsyscoop #boozyicecream

-Melissa Tavss

#BOOZYICECREAM

Filling pints in Hot Bread Kitchen,
Winter 2015

Grand opening of the flagship
Tipsy Scoop Barlour, Spring 2017

CHAPTER ONE

EQUIPMENT AND BASICS

EQUIPMENT

Before we get start taking you through recipe by recipe, spirit by spirit, we are going to go over some recommendations for equipment and kitchen tools that are must-haves for boozy ice cream making! Whether you are completely new to making ice cream or a seasoned pro, liquor-infused ice cream is a completely new beast - let's tackle it together!

To start, let's be reallllly honest with each other. How often are you planning on actually making our boozy ice creams? Or any ice cream for that matter?

Please take the following quiz so we can help you determine your level of commitment.

For dinner I usually:
a.) Order take out! Grubhub is King!
b.) Improvise a meal out of whatever nonsense I have in my fridge and hope it turns out to be delicious.
c.) Browse Recipes.com for a recipe I have never made before, then go to a specialty food store and pick up obscure ingredients. I will probably end up sous-vide-ing something.

 I watch cooking shows because:
a.) I am really hungry and there is nothing to eat.
b.) I WANT to cook - everything looks so delicious! But I'm a little lazy, so maybe on the weekend.
c.) I could be on a cooking show! Chopped is calling my name!

When I try a new yummy dessert I typically think:
a.) Get in my belly!
b.) I could make this! But it would definitely turn into a Pinterest fail.
c.) Is that buttercream or ganache?

If you answered mostly As, we know you are likely not going to be making too many of our recipes. Maybe you just bought this cookbook because the photos made you hungry and you thought the cover was like, really, really pretty - and that's okay!!! (Shameless plug: you can just order our ice creams for nationwide shipping on Goldbelly.com if you don't want to make them yourself!)

If you answered mostly Bs or Cs, you might actually make some of this stuff – and maybe even better than we do! Use our recipes as a baseline and customize them with your own tricks. We cannot wait to see what you come up with!

Based on your ice cream making commitment, we have different recommendations for ice-cream making equipment below. The most important thing we would advise is choosing a maker with a built-in compressor. We believe this is really important for boozy ice cream making as it allows for the ice cream to churn and freeze at the same time. The at-home ice cream makers that include a cylinder for freezing ahead of time just don't work as well. The ice cream sticks to the side of the cylinder when you take it out, which does not allow for a smooth, creamy consistency.

For a less serious ice cream chef: Cuisinart ICE-100 Compressor Ice Cream and Gelato Maker

For a serious ice cream chef: Lello 4080 Musso Lussino 1.5-Quart Ice Cream Maker, Stainless

The ice cream maker is obviously the most important piece of equipment in making boozy ice cream. Oh, and duh - the freezer! Make sure you have a working freezer!!!

If the ice in your your freezer is frozen, that means it works just fine. Remember to always store freshly made ice cream in the back of your freezer where it is coldest!

Here are some other tools you should have on hand to be able to make our recipes:

Kitchen tools checklist:
- Mixing bowl with at least 1-gallon capacity
- Medium size saucepan
- Measuring cups and spoons
- Gelato pan or freezer safe tubberware with at least 1-quart capacity
- Whisk
- Large kitchen spoon or spatula
- Knives
- Plastic wrap
- Food processor or blender

And now for the ice cream mix recipe...

ICE CREAM MIX

Our ice cream mix is the base for all of our liquor-infused ice cream flavors. With a high percentage of butterfat, this mix allows the ice cream to hold an alcohol content (up to 5% ABV) and still tastes creamy and delicious! Maintaining that adored ice cream consistency is extremely important to us. And of course, keeping those scoops tipsy is of serious concern!

1 1/2 cups Whole Milk
1 1/2 cups Heavy Cream
1 tablespoon Vanilla
1/3 cup Sugar
8 Egg Yolks

*Makes 1.5-2 quarts of ice cream mix

*Note: Our ice cream mix recipe has been adapted for a home chef. Actually, this is the ice cream mix recipe we started with since we were doing small 1.5-quart batches in the beginning! We no longer use eggs in our ice cream mix due to allergens and scalability, but we do think it's a great way to get the butterfat you need so the ice cream has the desired alcohol content and still stays creamy. We want you to end up with the Tipsy-est, most delicious scoops possible!

1. In a medium-sized heavy-duty saucepan, add milk, heavy cream, and vanilla. Over medium-high heat, scald the mixture, removing from heat once bubbles begin to form.
2. In a large bowl, add sugar and egg yolks and whisk until they turn a lighter yellow, about 30 seconds to 1 minute.
3. Slowly pour half of the scalded milk and cream mixture into the egg yolks, whisking constantly as you pour.
4. Add the milk and egg mixture back into the saucepan. Warm over low-to-medium heat, stirring constantly with a heat-resistant spatula or spoon. The custard is thick enough once it can easily coat a spatula or spoon, which takes a few minutes.
(Note: Overcooking will scramble the eggs, so proceed with caution.)
5. Transfer custard to a heat-proof container, cover, and let cool for 1 hour before adding in alcohol and additional ingredients.

CHOCOLATE ICE CREAM MIX

1 1/2 cups Whole Milk
1 1/2 cups Heavy Cream
1 tablespoon Vanilla
1/3 cup Sugar
8 egg Yolks
1/2 cup Cocoa Powder
1/2 cup Chocolate Chips
(Semi-Sweet or Dark)

*Makes 1.5-2 quarts of ice cream mix

1. In a medium-sized heavy-duty saucepan, add milk, heavy cream, cocoa powder and vanilla. Over medium-high heat, scald the mixture, removing from heat once bubbles begin to form.
2. Remove from heat and stir in chocolate chips until completely melted. Set aside.
3. In a large bowl, add sugar and egg yolks and whisk until they turn a lighter yellow, about 30 seconds to 1 minute. Slowly pour half of the scalded milk and cream mixture into the egg yolks, whisking constantly as you pour.
4. Add the milk and egg mixture back into the saucepan. Warm over low-to-medium heat, stirring constantly with a heat-resistant spatula or spoon. The custard is thick enough once it can easily coat a spatula or spoon, which takes a few minutes. (Note: Overcooking will scramble the eggs, so proceed with caution.)
5. Transfer custard to a heat-proof container, cover, and let cool for 1 hour before adding in alcohol and additional ingredients.

NON-DAIRY ICE CREAM AND SORBET

You'll notice in the chapters following that not only do we have milk-based ice creams, but also have a few options for non-dairy boozy ice creams and boozy sorbets! Our non-dairy ice creams are made with a coconut milk base and our sorbets are made with different fruits, so they have a water/fruit base.

Puree recipes vary fruit by fruit, but our sorbets all start with fruit purées- raspberry, mango, watermelon, peach etc. Since there is so much variation fruit by fruit, you'll see instructions for each fruit purée included within the recipes in the following chapters. What all sorbet recipes do have in common is the need for simple syrup. Here is a very simple, simple syrup recipe:

How to make simple syrup:

1 cup white sugar
1 cup water

In a medium saucepan, combine water and sugar. Bring to a boil, stirring, until sugar has dissolved. Allow it to cool.

> **PRO TIP:** We always recommend straining the seeds out when making fruit purées for sorbets and ice creams, this allows for a smoother consistency.

Now that we have covered all the basics, let's get started. Make sure to stock your home bar with the essentials: whiskey, bourbon, tequila, spiced rum, coconut rum, vodka, gin, beer, and wine. Think of yourself as an ice cream mixologist. It's like making cocktails, only in ice cream form. Think creatively, but also pay attention (lay off the ingredient taste testing a bit ;))- there are rules to make that Tipsy Scoop™!

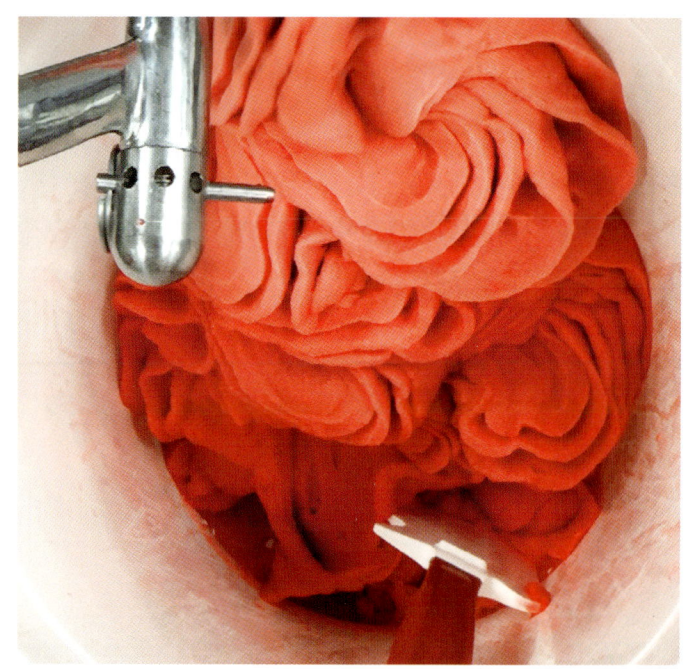

 @lifebysyd

CHAPTER TWO

WHISKEY AND BOURBON

DARK CHOCOLATE WHISKEY SALTED CARAMEL

Melissa wouldn't have labeled herself a whiskey fan when she came up with this flavor, but then she paired a dram of whiskey with a square of dark chocolate filled with salted caramel. Light bulb! The bitterness of the dark chocolate and sweet, salty taste of caramel made the whiskey go down so much smoother. You don't have to be a whiskey fiend to love this ice cream. But you might turn into one once we're done with you...

6 cups Chocolate Ice Cream Mix
(page 15)
2 tablespoons Salted Caramel Syrup
(we recommend Torani)
1 cup Whiskey

Makes about 2 quarts

SERVING SUGGESTION

Eat straight from the pint, standing in front of the freezer. Sometimes simple is best!

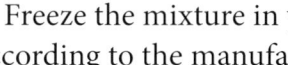

1. In large mixing bowl combine all the ingredients and stir.
2. Cover the bowl with plastic wrap and refrigerate for 1 to 2 hours.
3. Freeze the mixture in your ice cream maker according to the manufacturer's instructions, until it has a gelato-like consistency.
4. Transfer the ice cream into freezer-safe containers and freeze for at least 8 hours before serving.

@eating_longisland

DARK CHOCOLATE WHISKEY SALTED CARAMEL

LIQUOR-INFUSED Ice Cream

TIPSY SCOOP

ONE PINT (473 mL)

INGREDIENTS: PASTEURIZED
MILK, SUGAR, CORN SYRUP,
MONO AND DIGLYCERIDES,
BEAN GUM, CELLULOSE GUM,
CARRAGEENAN, WHISKEY,
XANTHAN GUM, VANILLA,
WITH POTASSIUM SORBATE,
NATURAL CARAMEL FLAVOR,

PROCESSED IN A FACILITY THAT USES

STORE ICE CREAM
IN THE BACK OF YOUR
FREEZER SET BELOW

STRAWBERRY RHUBARB BOURBON

When Rachel was growing up her grandmother would make the same strawberry rhubarb poundcake with cream cheese frosting for every big celebration. The rhubarb tartness of the moist cake was perfectly complimented by the sweet, cream cheese frosting. This is that cake in ice cream form—plus bourbon, of course. Customers see the pretty pink packaging and read "Strawberry Rhubarb," and expect this flavor to be as sweet and innocent as her grandmother's signature cake. At the end of the first bite, though...WOAH, bourbon. The soft, fruity ice cream allows the bourbon to show off even more than some of our other bourbon-infused flavors. You can't judge a boozy ice cream by its label...

Strawberry Purée:
2.5 pounds Fresh Strawberries
2 cups Simple Syrup
(Page 16)
1/4 cup Lemon Juice

Ice Cream:
4 cups Ice Cream Mix
(page 14)
1/2 cup Strawberry Purée
1 cup Four Roses Bourbon
1 tablespoon Rhubarb Bitters

Makes about 2 quarts

SERVING SUGGESTION

In a mason jar, top two large scoops with fancy granola, sweetened coconut flakes, and dried cranberries. Boo-zay parfait!

Make Purée:
1. Remove stems from strawberries.
2. Add lemon to simple syrup.
3. Place strawberries and simple syrup into blender or food processor until smooth.
4. Strain mixture with mesh strainer.
5. Let cool in fridge for at least one hour.

Make Ice Cream:
1. In large mixing bowl combine all the ingredients and stir.
2. Cover the bowl with plastic wrap and refrigerate for 1 to 2 hours.
3. Freeze the mixture in your ice cream maker according to the manufacturer's instructions, until it has a gelato-like consistency.
4. Transfer the ice cream into freezer-safe containers and freeze for at least 8 hours before serving.

MAPLE BACON BOURBON

From the city that mastered the art of boozy brunch, comes a flavor that is ideal for Saturday morning decadence. "Bacon in ice cream??" we are often asked. "Trust us," we respond. Bacon has found its way to donuts, cupcakes, and truffles, so why not ice cream? We start with our creamy vanilla bourbon ice cream base and then add a swirl of sweet maple syrup and chunks of crispy bacon. All of your favorite breakfast flavors in one salty-sweet bite. Bacon in ice cream--it's a bold move, but then again, so is booze in ice cream.

6 cups Ice Cream Mix
(page 14)
1 cup Four Roses Bourbon
1/4 cup Maple Syrup
1/2 cup Bacon, cooked & chopped

Makes about 2 quarts

SERVING SUGGESTION

Serve on top of a warm cinnamon roll and top with more bacon crumbles and a drizzle of maple syrup. Boozy. Bacony. Brunch.

1. In a large mixing bowl, combine ice cream mix, bourbon, and maple syrup and stir.
2. Cover the bowl with plastic wrap and refrigerate for 1 to 2 hours.
3. While mix chills, cook the bacon. You'll need 8-10 slices of raw bacon to make a 1/2 cup of crumbles (plus a few more for snacking...). Cook bacon until it is crispy and set aside on a paper towel to drain and cool for around 30 minutes. Chop into quarter-inch pieces using a sharp knife. Refrigerate in airtight container until ready to add to ice cream.
4. Freeze the mixture in your ice cream maker according to the manufacturer's instructions, until it has a gelato-like consistency.
5. Transfer the ice cream to a large mixing bowl and stir in bacon crumbles.
6. Transfer the ice cream into freezer-safe containers and freeze for at least 8 hours before serving.

PB AND J OLD FASHIONED

By now you know how we feel about perfect pairings. Now let's talk about the ultimate pairing-Peanut Butter and Jelly! Our PB&J Old Fashioned ice cream is a grown up take on this childhood classic. We start by infusing peanut butter ice cream with whisky, and then we swirl in fresh strawberry purée. Peanut butter meets jelly meets whisky. Rich, savory ice cream meets tart, refreshing fruit. If this flavor was in your lunch box, you wouldn't trade it for anything.

6 cups Ice Cream Mix
(page 14)
1 cup Monkey Shoulder Whisky
1/2 cup Peanut Butter
(melted and slightly cooled)
1/4 cup Strawberry Purée
(page 22)

Makes about 3 quarts

SERVING SUGGESTION

Top with French Toast Crunch cereal, strawberry sauce, and gummy strawberries and serve in a red bowl. PB&J Sundae!

1. In a large mixing bowl, combine ice cream mix, whisky, and melted peanut butter and stir.
2. Cover the bowl with plastic wrap and refrigerate for 1 to 2 hours.
3. Freeze mixture in your ice cream maker according to the manufacturer's instructions, until it has a gelato-like consistency.
4. Transfer the ice cream into an oversized freezer safe container (with enough room to swirl in the strawberry purée later).
5. Allow ice cream to freeze for at least 4 hours in the back of the freezer, until firm to the touch but not totally frozen.
6. Use a spoon to swirl strawberry purée into the ice cream. Do not blend purée entirely into ice cream; it should maintain a swirled appearance.
7. Transfer the ice cream into freezer-safe containers and freeze for at least 8 hours before serving.

@thisgirleatsny

SANTA'S COOKIES N WHISKY

The older you get, the more you realize Santa could definitely use something a little stronger than milk and cookies. Doesn't the guy deserve a little nip of whisky to warm up between houses? Our grown-up take starts with our signature vanilla ice cream spiked with whisky, and then incorporates chunks of chocolate chip cookies (freshly baked if you're up for it... or store-bought if not). Making this ice cream will quickly become a favorite holiday tradition, and if you're the "Santa" at your house, you totally deserve this.

6 cups Ice Cream Mix
(page 14)
1 cup Maker's Mark Bourbon Whisky
1 1/2 cups Crumbled Chocolate Chip
Cookies, homemade or store-bought

Makes about 2 quarts

SERVING SUGGESTION

Make the ultimate cookie lover's sundae with Santa's Cookies N Whisky ice cream, cookie crumble, chocolate fudge and a maraschino cherry! Add a boozy ice cream sandwich (page 88) on top and you're guaranteed to be on the nice list.

1. In a large mixing bowl, combine the ice cream mix and whisky and stir.
2. Cover the bowl with plastic wrap and refrigerate for 1 to 2 hours.
3. Freeze the mixture in your ice cream maker according to the manufacturer's instructions, until it has a gelato-like consistency.
4. Transfer the ice cream to a large mixing bowl and stir in the crumbled cookies.
5. Transfer the ice cream into freezer-safe containers and freeze for at least 8 hours before serving.

CHAPTER THREE

TEQUILA

SPIKED HAZELNUT COFFEE

The original name for this flavor was "Boozy Affogato," to bring to mind the traditional Italian dessert in which a scoop of vanilla ice cream is topped (or "drowned") with a shot of hot espresso. As it turns out, most people don't know what an affogato is, so we decided to keep it straightforward (alcohol-infused ice cream is unique enough, after all). Our recipe mixes Patrón XO Café (a coffee tequila liqueur) with hazelnut liqueur, but we encourage you to adapt to fit your taste, just as you would your morning coffee. Want a stronger coffee flavor? Add chilled espresso instead of cold brew. Or make a frozen caffè mocha by swapping hazelnut liqueur for chocolate. No matter how you take it, there's no better way to get buzzed.

6 cups Ice Cream Mix
(page 14)
1/4 cup Cold Brew Coffee
1 cup Patrón XO Café
1/4 cup Hazelnut Liqueur

Makes about 2 quarts

SERVING SUGGESTION

Stir into your morning coffee or espresso to make a boozy affogato (we'll never give up!) More boozy affogato recipes on page 86.

1. In a large mixing bowl combine all ingredients and stir.
2. Cover the bowl with plastic wrap and refrigerate for 1 to 2 hours.
3. Freeze the mixture in your ice cream maker according to the manufacturer's instructions, until it has a gelato-like consistency.
4. Transfer the ice cream into freezer-safe container and freeze for at least 8 hours before serving.

TEQUILA MEXICAN "HOT" CHOCOLATE

When you think of tequila-based cocktails, you think refreshing- palomas and margaritas, like the sorbets later in this chapter. But tequila is also perfect for a rich, decadent, end-of-night drink that's actually dessert in disguise. In this recipe, chocolate ice cream receives a healthy dose of tequila and then an extra kick from cinnamon.

6 cups Chocolate Ice Cream Mix
(page 15)
1 cup Altos Tequila Plata
1/4 cup Cinnamon

Makes about 2 quarts

SERVING SUGGESTION

Scoop into your favorite mug and top with whipped cream and mini marshmallows. Garnish with a cinnamon stick.

1. In a large mixing bowl combine all ingredients and stir.
2. Cover the bowl with plastic wrap and refrigerate for 1 to 2 hours.
3. Freeze the mixture in your ice cream maker according to the manufacturer's instructions, until it has a gelato-like consistency.
4. Transfer the ice cream into freezer-safe container and freeze for at least 8 hours before serving.

PRO TIP : For a more adventurous option add a tablespoon of chile liqueur like Ancho Reyes (in addition to the tequila), and spice things up even more!

 @52chefs

MANGO MARGARITA SORBET

Is there anything more fun than frozen margaritas? After a few too many happy hours, we knew we had to make a margarita-inspired sorbet that was just as refreshing, addictive, and potentially lethal as the real deal. Our adaptation uses Altos Tequila Reposado and fresh mango, which provides us with a much-needed tropical escape during the cold New York winters. No matter if there's still dirty snow on the ground or many more weeks of winter on the horizon, a margarita at happy hour temporarily transports you to a warm, sandy beach. And if you're like us, you won't be able to stop at just one...

Mango Purée:
2 cups Simple Syrup
(page 16)
3 cups Fresh Mango, diced

Sorbet:
4 cups Mango Purée
1 cup Altos Tequila Reposado
1 cup Filtered Water
1 tablespoon Lime Juice

Makes about 2 quarts

SERVING SUGGESTION

Scoop into a salt or sugar rimmed margarita glass and garnish with tropical fruit. For more fun add an extra a shot of tequila on top.

Make Purée:
1. Purée diced mango in blender or food processor until smooth. Set aside.
2. In a large mixing bowl, combine mango and simple syrup and stir.

Make Sorbet:
1. Stir in tequila, lime juice and filtered water into bowl with mango purée.
2. Cover the bowl with plastic wrap and refrigerate for 1 to 2 hours.
3. Freeze the mixture in your ice cream maker according to the manufacturer's instructions.
4. Transfer the sorbet into freezer-safe container and freeze for at least 8 hours before serving.

 @sublime.eats

WATERMELON MINT MARGARITA SORBET

Watermelon. Mint. Margarita. Is there a more mouthwatering combination of words in the whole English language?? This sorbet is sitting on the back porch with a juicy slice of watermelon dripping down your forearm. It's cutting out of work early for a happy hour margarita on that first really hot day of summer. It's a drippy cone of mint chocolate chip ice cream after dinner on a surprisingly great first date. We could go on, but just make it and see for yourself...

Watermelon Purée:
2 cups Simple Syrup
(page 16)
3 cups Fresh Watermelon Chunks

Sorbet:
4 cups Watermelon Purée
1 cup Tequila
1/3 cup Mint Syrup
(we recommend Monin)
1/4 cup Lemon Juice

Makes about 2 quarts

SERVING SUGGESTION

Recreate our Watermelon Mint Margarita Sundae by using an ice cream disher to scoop the sorbet into a pink cone bowl and garnish with fresh mint, Watermelon Jelly Bean "seeds," and sour watermelon gummies.

Make Purée:
1. Remove seeds from watermelon and purée in blender or food processor until smooth. Set aside.
2. In a large mixing bowl, combine watermelon with simple syrup and stir.

Make Sorbet:
1. Combine watermelon purée with tequila, mint syrup, and lemon juice.
2. Cover the bowl with plastic wrap and refrigerate for 1 to 2 hours.
3. Freeze the mixture in your ice cream maker according to the manufacturer's instructions.
4. Transfer the sorbet into freezer-safe container and freeze for at least 8 hours before serving.

 @lifebysyd

CHAPTER
FOUR

"HOT" BUTTERED RUM

What could be better than that last bite in your bowl of Cinnamon Toast Crunch? That cinnamon-y sweet cereal milk bite is absolutely divine. But how about we SPIKE that and make it into an ice cream? We are all ears! For your Cinnamon Toast Crunch infused milk- all grown up, try making our "Hot" Buttered Rum ice cream. Not only will it give you that taste of nostalgia, but will bring you that festive, comforting, holiday party in your mouth feeling all year long.

6 cups Ice Cream Mix
(page 14)
1/4 cup Cinnamon
1 tablespoon Melted Butter
1 cup Sailor Jerry Spiced Rum

Makes about 2 quarts

SERVING SUGGESTION

Serve in a cereal bowl and garnish with Cinnamon Toast Crunch, rainbow sprinkles and cherries.

1. In a large mixing bowl combine all the ingredients and stir.
2. Cover the bowl with plastic wrap and refrigerate for 1 to 2 hours.
3. Freeze the mixture in your ice cream maker according to the manufacturer's instructions, until it has a gelato-like consistency.
4. Transfer the ice cream into freezer-safe containers and freeze for at least 8 hours before serving.

THE INSIDE SCOOP ON SPICED RUM:
Legend has it, the term "proof" comes from the method sailors used to assure their rum rations weren't being watered down. The ship's captain would ladle out a sample of the day's rum barrel in front of the men and douse it with gunpowder, then give it a spark! If the rum was full strength the powder would ignite, giving the sailors "proof" of the integrity of their rum!

BOOZY BANANAS FOSTER

How is Bananas Foster seriously considered a meal?? We don't really care, we're just happy this dessert can be disguised as breakfast without anyone giving you a hard time! For those of you that don't partake in this delicious brunch treat, it's caramelized bananas flambéed in rum, and often served à la mode. Our Boozy Bananas Foster ice cream incorporates all of these divine flavors into one heavenly scoop.

6 cups Ice Cream Mix
(page 14)
2 tablespoons Brown Sugar
2 tablespoons Crème De Banana Liqueur
1 cup Sailor Jerry Spiced Rum

Makes about 2 quarts

SERVING SUGGESTION

Caramelize sliced bananas and make a bananas foster split! Add extra toppings like hot fudge, caramel sauce, toffee, walnuts and more.

1. In a large mixing bowl, combine all ingredients and stir.
2. Cover the bowl with plastic wrap and refrigerate for 1 to 2 hours.
3. Freeze the mixture in your ice cream maker according to the manufacturer's instructions, until it has a gelato-like consistency.
4. Transfer the ice cream into freezer-safe containers and freeze for at least 8 hours before serving.

SPIKED SPICED PUMPKIN PIE

Thanksgiving is all about being thankful for food, booze and family – in no particular order. It's also a great time to embrace stretchy pants, the imminent food coma, and NOT the time to say no to dessert. We decided to upgrade the Thanksgiving dessert favorite, pumpkin pie, into a creamy, pumpkin-y, rum-infused scoop!

6 cups Ice Cream Mix
(page 14)
1/4 cup Pumpkin Purée
1 1/2 tablespoons Cinnamon
1 cup Sailor Jerry Spiced Rum

Makes about 2 quarts

SERVING SUGGESTION

Make a boozy ice cream pie! Fill a homemade or store bought pie crust with ice cream and then top with walnuts, graham cracker crumble, and a drizzle of caramel. Place candy pumpkins along the rim of the crust.

1. In a large mixing bowl, combine all ingredients and stir.
2. Cover the bowl with plastic wrap and refrigerate for 1 to 2 hours.
3. Freeze the mixture in your ice cream maker according to the manufacturer's instructions, until it has a gelato-like consistency.
4. Transfer the ice cream into freezer-safe containers and freeze for at least 8 hours before serving.

 @feedyourgirlfriend

PIÑA COLADA

If you like Piña Coladasssss... Is that even a valid question, Rupert Holmes?? Is there anything that tastes more like vacation? Transport yourself to that dream tropical island with this creamy pineapple ice cream infused with coconut rum!

2 cups Simple Syrup
(page 16)
1/2 cup Pineapple Chunks
1 cup Coconut Milk
1 cup Malibu Original Rum

Makes about 2 quarts

SERVING SUGGESTION

Hollow out a pineapple and then fill the inside with Piña Colada ice cream-that's aggressive and cool, and we like it! Garnish with coconut flakes and a drink umbrella.

1. Purée fresh pineapple chunks in a blender or food processor until smooth.
2. In a large mixing bowl combine puréed pineapple with coconut milk and whisk together.
3. Add simple syrup and Malibu Original Rum and stir.
4. Cover the bowl with plastic wrap and refrigerate for 1 to 2 hours.
5. Freeze the mixture in your ice cream maker according to the manufacturer's instructions, until it has a gelato-like consistency.
6. Transfer the ice cream into freezer-safe containers and freeze for at least 8 hours before serving.

PRO TIP: Ditch the coconut rum and make it virgin! Pregnant women and children rejoice!

CHAPTER
FIVE

VODKA

CAKE BATTER VODKA MARTINI

This one takes the cake (batter)! And really just makes your martini that much more bearable and way less toxic. Say RIP Fake ID and indulge in this fan favorite. Our Cake Batter Vodka Martini ice cream is the perfect cocktail turned dessert. Rainbow sprinkles are a must here. Whether you are celebrating your 21st birthday or your 21st birthday plus 10 or 15 or 20 or 25...

6 cups Ice Cream Mix
(page 14)
1/2 cup Whipped Cream Vodka
1/4 cup Amaretto
1/4 cup White Chocolate Liqueur

Makes about 2 quarts

SERVING SUGGESTION

Make a boozy ice cream cake!!!
See page 90 for instructions!

1. In a large mixing bowl combine all ingredients and stir.
2. Cover the bowl with plastic wrap and refrigerate for 1 to 2 hours.
3. Freeze the mixture in your ice cream maker according to the manufacturer's instructions, until it has a gelato-like consistency.
4. Transfer the ice cream into freezer-safe container and freeze for at least 8 hours before serving.

CANDY CANE VODKA MARTINI

This is not your college Christmas party peppermint patty shot. Tacky sweaters and cheap chocolate syrup need not apply. While mint-infused desserts always run the risk of being too minty, here peppermint-infused vodka and crushed candy cane are delicately folded into our rich vanilla ice cream for a mint flavor that's refreshing without being overpowering. Plus, this infused vodka is a pretty and cost-effective gift for the spirit lovers on your list. Nice, but still a little naughty...

Candy Cane-Infused Vodka:
1 cup Vodka
5 Full Sized Candy Canes,
broken into 1-inch pieces

Ice Cream:
6 cups Ice Cream Mix
(page 14)
1 cup Candy Cane Infused Vodka
1/4 cup Peppermint Schnapps
5 Full-Sized Candy Canes, crushed

Makes about 2 quarts

SERVING SUGGESTION

For an easy holiday dinner party dessert, scoop into small glass bowls and top with whipped cream, a sprinkle of crushed candy cane, and a maraschino cherry.

Make Candy Cane Vodka:
1. Combine the vodka and candy cane pieces in a mason jar.
2. Store in a cool, dark place for 24 hours, shaking occasionally to disperse candy cane pieces.

Make Ice Cream:
1. In a large mixing bowl, combine candy cane-infused vodka, ice cream mix, and peppermint schnapps and stir.
2. Cover the bowl with plastic wrap and refrigerate for 1 to 2 hours.
3. Freeze the mixture in your ice cream maker according to the manufacturer's instructions.
4. Once the ice cream has a gelato-like consistency, transfer to a large mixing bowl and stir in the crushed candy canes.
5. Transfer the ice cream into freezer-safe containers and freeze for at least 8 hours before serving.

MOSCOW MULE "ENDLESS SUMMER"

Spoiler alert: We LOVE summer. It's the best season for eating ice cream, drinking outside- SO many of our favorite activities. We wanted to make a flavor to help us hold onto those fleeting days of September summer when vacations are officially over and mornings are starting to get a little bit chilly. This recipe features fresh lime juice, coconut milk, and Absolut® Lime for a tangy non-dairy ice cream perfect for those still-hot September afternoons. The little kick of spice from ginger beer is a reminder that jackets and colds are just around the corner—savor every bite of summer.

2 cups Simple Syrup
(page 16)
1 cup Coconut Milk
1 1/2 cups Fresh Lime Juice
1 cup Absolut® Lime Vodka
1/2 cup Ginger Beer

Makes about 2 quarts

1. In a large mixing bowl combine all ingredients and stir.
2. Cover the bowl with plastic wrap and refrigerate for 1 to 2 hours.
3. Freeze in your ice cream maker according to the manufacturer's instructions, until it has a gelato-like consistency.
4. Transfer the ice cream into freezer-safe containers and freeze for at least 8 hours before serving.

SERVING SUGGESTION

Recreate our Moscow Mule "Endless Summer" Sundae by scooping ice cream into a copper Moscow Mule mug and garnishing with fresh mint, lime, rock candy "ice," and a gummy lime wedge.

STRAWBERRY KISS MARTINI

Nothing says Valentine's Day quite like chocolate covered strawberries. Whether you are in love with a real human being, a reality star crush, chocolate, or just vodka – we have the perfect treat that will really win over their heart once and for all.

6 cups Ice Cream Mix
(page 14)
1/4 cup Strawberry Purée
(page 22)
1 cup Whipped Cream Vodka
1/4 cup Semi-Sweet Chocolate Chips

Makes about 2 quarts

SERVING SUGGESTION

Serve in a champagne coupe and top with prosecco. Garnish with fresh a slice of fresh strawberry.

1. In a large mixing bowl, combine ice cream mix, vodka and strawberry purée and stir.
2. Cover the bowl with plastic wrap and refrigerate for 1 to 2 hours.
3. Freeze the mixture in your ice cream maker according to the manufacturer's instructions.
4. Once the ice cream has a gelato-like consistency, transfer to a large mixing bowl and stir in the chocolate chips.
5. Transfer the ice cream into freezer-safe containers and freeze for at least 8 hours before serving.

CHAPTER SIX

LIQUEURS
AND
MORE

RHUBARB GIN AND GINGER

When you're contacted by the PR team for the British government and asked to develop a custom boozy ice cream for British Wine & Spirits Week, you say yes, obviously. Will it be a bit stressful when the gin is held up at customs causing production delays on a project that already has a very quick turnaround? Sure. But the end result will make it all worth it. This delicately fruity, intensely flavorful ice cream easily secured a spot on our list of all-time favorite custom flavors.

6 cups Ice Cream Mix
(page 14)
1 cup Whitley Neill Gin Rhubarb & Ginger
2 tablespoon Ginger Syrup
(we recommend Monin)
OR 2 tablespoons Grated Fresh Ginger
2 teaspoons Vanilla Extract

Makes about 2 quarts

SERVING SUGGESTION

Scoop into small sugar cones and garnish with edible flowers and rainbow sprinkles.

1. In a large mixing bowl combine all ingredients and stir.
2. Cover the bowl with plastic wrap and refrigerate for 1 to 2 hours.
3. Freeze the mixture in your ice cream maker according to the manufacturer's instructions, until it has a gelato-like consistency.
4. Transfer the ice cream into freezer-safe containers and freeze for at least 8 hours before serving.

RASPBERRY LIMONCELLO SORBET

Raspberry Limoncello is the most obviously ITALIAN of our flavors. Limoncello, an Italian lemon liqueur, is traditionally served chilled as an after-dinner digestivo. In Italy, you'll find limoncello in cocktails, pastries, gelato, or simply served by the glass. It's far less prevalent in the States, and this flavor is our small effort to change that. Refreshing but decadent, tart with a balancing sweetness, this sorbet makes us feel like we're sitting on the terrace of an Italian villa sipping a cocktail. While our whiskey and vodka flavors steal most of the attention, the Raspberry Limoncello Sorbet keeps us in touch with our roots.

Raspberry Purée:
6 cups Raspberries
1 cup Simple Syrup
(page 16)
2 tablespoons Fresh Lemon Juice

Sorbet:
2 cup Limoncello
1 cup Filtered Water
6 cups Raspberry Purée

Makes about 2 quarts

SERVING SUGGESTION

Scoop Raspberry Limoncello Sorbet into a cordial glass and pour over chilled Limoncello. Garnish with a single fresh raspberry and a thin strip of lemon peel. Sit back and feel very Italian.

Make Purée:
1. Purée the raspberries, simple syrup, and lemon juice in a blender or food processor until smooth.
2. Strain the mixture through a fine sieve into a large mixing bowl. Press down with a rubber spatula to extract as much liquid as possible.

Make Sorbet:
1. Stir in limoncello and filtered water into bowl with raspberry purée.
2. Cover the bowl with plastic wrap and refrigerate for 1-2 hours.
3. Freeze the mixture in your ice cream maker according to the manufacturer's instructions.
4. Transfer the sorbet into freezer-safe containers and freeze for at least 8 hours before serving.

 @music2mymouth

NEGRONI CREAMSICLE

The classic Negroni is simple, but lethal—equal parts gin, vermouth, and Campari garnished with an orange peel. The bitterness imparted by Campari is mellowed by sweet vermouth, but remains the standout flavor in the cocktail. In this recipe we mix in even more bitterness with the addition of fresh grapefruit, but then balance things out with a sweet coconut milk base. Serve this non-dairy creamcicle as light, summertime dessert, or as a mid-afternoon aperitivo, just as you would its namesake.

2 cups Simple Syrup
(page 16)
1 1/2 cups Grapefruit Juice
(approximately 2 large grapefruits)
1 cup Coconut Milk
1/4 cup Gin
1/4 cup Dry Vermouth
1/4 cup Campari

Makes about 2 quarts

SERVING SUGGESTION

Scoop two large, rounded scoops into a rocks glass. Garnish with a grapefruit wedge.

1. Cut the grapefruits in half with a sharp knife. Using a handheld citrus reamer, twist the flesh of the grapefruit on the reamer to extract the juice. Strain the liquid for less pulp.
2. In a large mixing bowl combine the grapefruit juice, simple syrup, and coconut milk and whisk together.
3. Add the gin, vermouth, and Campari and stir to combine.
4. Cover the bowl with plastic wrap and refrigerate for 1 to 2 hours.
5. Freeze the mixture in your ice cream maker according to the manufacturer's instructions, until it has a gelato-like consistency.
6. Transfer the ice cream into freezer-safe containers and freeze for at least 8 hours before serving.

SALTED CARAMEL APPLE BRANDY

An apple ice cream a day keeps the doctor away! This light (but decadent) fruit-filled flavor will quickly become your go-to dessert during apple season. PLUS, the caramel apple mix, which could honestly be a dessert on it's own, makes it ridiculously easy to fit in an extra serving of fruit after dinner. You're welcome.

Caramel Apples:

3 Medium Granny Smith Apples
2 tablespoons Butter
1/4 cup Brown Sugar
1 teaspoon Cinnamon
1 tablespoon Store Bought Caramel

Ice Cream:

6 cups Ice Cream Mix
(page 14)
2 tablespoons Salted Caramel Syrup
(we recommend Torani)
1 cup Torres Brandy
1 cup Caramel Apples

Makes about 2 quarts

SERVING SUGGESTION

Top ice cream with leftover caramel apples and graham cracker crumble. Apple pie meets boozy ice cream!

 @lifebysyd

Make Caramel Apples:

1. Wash, peel, and core apples and chop into 1/2 inch pieces.
2. Melt two tablespoons over medium heat and then stir in the brown sugar.
3. Add apples and cinnamon and cook until apples are softened and most of the liquid has evaporated, 10 to 15 minutes.
4. Remove from heat and let cool for 5 minutes. Stir in salted caramel syrup.
Store in refrigerator until ready to use in the ice cream.

Make Ice Cream:

1. In a large mixing bowl, combine ice cream mix, Torres Brandy, and salted caramel syrup.
2. Cover the bowl with plastic wrap and refrigerate for 1 to 2 hours.
3. Freeze the mixture in your ice cream maker according to the manufacturer's instructions, until it has a gelato-like consistency.
4. Transfer the ice cream to a large mixing bowl and stir in caramel apples.
5. Transfer the ice cream into freezer-safe containers and freeze for at least 8 hours before serving.

CHAPTER SEVEN

BEER
AND
WINE

CHOCOLATE STOUT & SALTY PRETZEL

Ahhh the salty sweet combo...is there anything better than adding a salty crunch to a chocolate-based dessert? This perfect pairing was the inspiration for our first ever beer-infused ice cream, Chocolate Stout & Salty Pretzel. As every beer lover knows, stouts are often described as having notes of chocolate, which make them the obvious choice for spiking chocolate ice cream. When choosing a stout to use in this recipe, we recommend deciding based on your sweet tooth. A dry Irish Stout like Guinness will produce a malty, mildly-sweet ice cream, while a higher ABV chocolate stout like Brooklyn Brewery Black Chocolate will make a sweeter, boozier ice cream. No matter your choice, the result will be as refreshing as a cold beer on a hot day.

6 cups Chocolate Ice Cream Mix
(page 15)
2 cups Brooklyn Brewery Black
Chocolate Stout
3/4 cup Crushed Pretzels

Makes about 2 quarts

SERVING SUGGESTION
Serve a large scoop on top of a warm, soft pretzel. Drizzle with chocolate syrup.

1. In a large mixing bowl combine ice cream mix and Brooklyn Brewery Black Chocolate Stout and stir.
2. Cover the bowl with plastic wrap and refrigerate for 1 to 2 hours.
3. Freeze the mixture in your ice cream maker according to the manufacturer's instructions, until it has a gelato-like consistency.
4. Transfer the ice cream into a large mixing bowl and stir in crushed pretzels.
5. Transfer the ice cream into freezer-safe containers and freeze for at least 8 hours before serving.

BOILERMAKER

Some call it a "Beer/Shot Combo," others call it "When in Brooklyn," but the Merriam Webster definition for a shot of whiskey served with a glass of beer is a "Boilermaker." Not only does this combination make for an excellent Happy Hour special, it also creates a fluffy, decadent ice cream flavor. As opposed to our Chocolate Stout & Salty Pretzel ice cream, we use a vanilla base in this recipe to allow both the caramel sweetness of the whiskey and roasty notes of the stout to shine through. Bottoms up!

6 cups Ice Cream Mix
(page 14)
1 cup Stout Beer
1/4 cup Whiskey

Makes about 2 quarts

SERVING SUGGESTION

Perfect á la mode! Serve a scoop on top of a brownie or cookie skillet and drizzle with chocolate fudge.

1. In a large mixing bowl combine all ingredients and stir.
2. Cover the bowl with plastic wrap and refrigerate for 1 to 2 hours.
3. Freeze the mixture in your ice cream maker according to the manufacturer's instructions, until it has a gelato-like consistency.
4. Transfer the ice cream into freezer-safe containers and freeze for at least 8 hours before serving.

@mikebakesnyc

BLOOD ORANGE CHAMPAGNE SPARKLER SORBET

Blood oranges are only in season for a few months of the year, so this is one of our most anticipated flavors. After Thanksgiving we can't wait to start making this tangy, dairy-free favorite, that's just as pretty as it is delicious. Our go-to serving suggestion for our sorbets is to pour over sparkling wine or champagne and make a simple float. That pairing was born here! The only thing better than spooning this refreshing sorbet straight from the ice cream machine into your mouth is allowing it to freeze the full 8 hours (so torturous!) and then serving it in a champagne flute drowned in bubbly. Is it just us, or does anticipation actually make food taste better?

2 cups Simple Syrup
(page 16)
2 cups Freshly Squeezed Blood Orange
Juice (4-5 large blood oranges)
1 cup Champagne
2 cups Filtered Water

Makes about 2 quarts

SERVING SUGGESTION

Champagne flute + Sorbet + more
Champagne on top. Done.

1. If the oranges are firm, first roll them on the countertop while applying downward pressure.
2. Cut the oranges in half and use a citrus reamer to extract the juice. Strain the liquid if you prefer no pulp.
3. In a large mixing bowl combine blood orange juice with other ingredients and stir.
4. Cover the bowl with plastic wrap and refrigerate for 1-2 hours.
5. Freeze the mixture in your ice cream maker according to the manufacturer's instructions.
6. Transfer the sorbet into freezer-safe containers and freeze for at least 8 hours before serving.

FROSÉ ALL DAY SORBET

Every summer there's a new cocktail trend. Aperol Spritz fountains. Rosé 40s. Cocktails that fit your juice cleanse. Some trends, like frosé, are good enough to stand the test of time. Frosé has secured its spot on summertime menus everywhere- from the frozen drink machine at your neighborhood dive, to a staple cocktail at boozy brunch, to our list of recurring seasonal flavors. You just can't get more refreshing then a sorbet made with fresh white peaches and infused with a crisp, fruit-forward rosé. "Frosé all day" isn't just a slightly overused, though undeniably catchy, saying-during summer, it's a way of life.

Peach Purée:
2 cups Simple Syrup
(page 16)
8 Ripe Peaches, peeled and sliced

Sorbet:
4 cups Peach Purée
1 cup Dry Rosé Wine
1 cup Filtered Water
1/4 cup Lemon Juice

Makes about 2 quarts

SERVING SUGGESTION

Make a Frosé sundae by placing two large scoops of the fully frozen sorbet in a pink cone bowl or standard bowl. Top with gummy peach rings, rosé gummies, edible rose petals, and a maraschino cherry.

Make Purée:
1. Purée peaches in blender or food processor until smooth. Set aside.
2. In a large mixing bowl, combine peaches, simple syrup and lemon juice and stir.

Make Sorbet:
1. Stir rosé and filtered water into bowl with peach purée.
2. Cover the bowl with plastic wrap and refrigerate for 1 to 2 hours.
3. Freeze the mixture in your ice cream maker according to the manufacturer's instructions.
4. Transfer the sorbet into freezer-safe containers and freeze for at least 8 hours before serving.

 @feedyourgirlfriend

CHAPTER EIGHT

BEYOND
THE SCOOP

NIGHT OWL

The older you get, the harder it is to stay up late enough to hit those trendy new cocktail bars. So we came up with a drink to help you make it to last call (or at least to first call) The Night Owl features our Spiked Hazelnut Coffee ice cream with cold brew coffee and Duclaw Sweet Baby Jesus! Chocolate Peanut Butter Porter. Feeling just fine with your current bedtime? Call it dessert. But on those nights when you feel like closing down the bar, mix up a Night Owl.

Spiked Hazelnut Coffee Ice Cream
(page 32)
Wandering Bear Cold Brew
Duclaw Sweet Baby Jesus! Chocolate
Peanut Butter Porter
Patrón XO Café (optional)

1. Pour 5 ounces porter and 5 ounces cold brew into a mason jar.
2. Slowly add one scoop of ice cream.
3. Insert colorful paper straw and long bar spoon.
4. Add another scoop ice cream and drizzle with chocolate syrup.
5. Optional: Make it boozier by mixing in a shot of Patrón XO Café before adding the ice cream!

 @feedyourgirlfriend

PARTY LIKE IT'S YOUR BIRTHDAY

Recipe for the perfect birthday: Cake + Ice Cream + LOTS of prosecco. You can add more ingredients, like breakfast in bed or dancing on tables, but those first three are non-negotiable! This pretty cocktail will make you feel like you're partying like its your birthday even on a boring Tuesday night when you're just catching up on work and watching bad reality TV. We suggest keeping the prosecco bottle close so you can top yourself off one, or two, or three times...

2 scoops Cake Batter Vodka Martini Ice Cream (page 52)
4 ounces Prosecco
1 ounce Vodka
Rainbow Nonpareils
Lime
Champagne Coupe
Birthday Cake Gummy

> **PRO TIP:** Use a mini bottle of prosecco when making this drink! Add the 4 ounces of bubbly to the cocktail and then serve the remainder of the bottle on the side. You can add more as you go!

1. Using a lime wedge, run the notch all around the front of the glass until it is very wet with lime juice.
2. Roll on a plate of nonpareils until side of glass is coated.
3. Scoop one small scoop of ice cream into glass
4. Pour 1 ounce of vodka into the glass.
5. Fill glass about 3/4 to top with prosecco.
6. Add another small scoop of ice cream to glass.
7. Add more sprinkles to the top scoop.
8. Garnish with birthday cake gummy and paper straw.

 @feedyourgirlfriend

BOOZY AFFOGATOS

As you know, we are VERY into affogatos. The traditional Italian dessert featuring ice cream drenched in espresso was the inspiration behind one of our first flavors, Spiked Hazelnut Coffee. Truly the only thing that makes the combo of coffee and ice cream better is booze. Below we give you some of our favorite boozy affogato combinations, but feel free to experiment with your own flavor pairings! If you come up with a buzzworthy combo, we'd love to hear it. Tag us @tipsyscoop on Instagram and maybe your idea will appear in our next book (with credit, of course!)

ESPRESSO AT HOME: If you have your very own fancy espresso machine at home, you're in luck! If not, you can make "espresso" at home using a drip coffee maker. Using finely ground, dark roast coffee beans, prepare coffee as you normally would, but increase the amount of ground coffee beans in the basket; we suggest around 3 tablespoons of coffee per 6 ounces of water.

Classic Spiked Hazelnut Coffee Affogato:
Put 2 small scoops Spiked Hazelnut Coffee ice cream (page 32) into a small coffee mug. Pour over 1 ounce hazelnut liqueur and 2 ounces espresso.

Irish Coffee:
Put 2 small scoops Boilermaker ice cream (page 74) into a clear, glass Irish Coffee mug. Pour over 2 ounces hot espresso, 1 ounce Whiskey and 1 ounce Bailey's Original Irish Cream. Garnish with whipped cream and chocolate shavings.

Boozy Peppermint Mocha:
Put 2 small scoops Candy Cane Vodka Martini ice cream (page 54) into your favorite Christmas mug and drizzle with chocolate syrup. Pour over 1 ounce Peppermint Schnapps and 2 ounces hot espresso. Garnish with whipped cream and crushed peppermint.

BOOZY ICE CREAM SANDWICHES

Ice cream sandwiches are the best kind of sandwiches in our humble opinion. Add a little booze and they're that much better! Bake the cookies yourself using your tried and true recipe, or keep it easy and pick them up from your favorite bakery. They're really just a vehicle for eating as much boozy ice cream as possible.

Spiked Hazelnut Coffee + Chocolate Chip Cookie Sandwiches

Spiked Hazelnut Coffee Ice Cream
(page 32)
Chocolate Chip Cookies
(around 3 inches in diameter)

1. If cookies are fresh baked, freeze for 30-40 minutes before assembling so they won't melt the ice cream.
2. Using an ice cream scoop, make a rounded scoop (about 3oz) of Spiked Hazelnut Coffee ice cream and place onto one cookie. Top with second cookie and press down lightly to adhere.
3. Enjoy immediately or store in freezer safe container
4. Optional: Make it an adult chipwich! Roll sides of sandwich in mini chocolate chips.

Cake Batter Vodka Martini + Funfetti Cookie Sandwiches

Cake Batter Vodka Martini Ice Cream
(page 52)
Funfetti Cookies
(around 3 inches in diameter)

1. If cookies are fresh baked, freeze for 30-40 minutes before assembling so they won't melt the ice cream.
2. Using an ice cream scoop, make a rounded scoop (about 3oz) of Cake Batter Vodka Martini ice cream and place onto one cookie. Top with second cookie and press down lightly to adhere.
3. Enjoy immediately or store in freezer safe container
4. Optional: Roll sides of sandwich in rainbow sprinkles

BOOZY ICE CREAM CAKES

Whether you're saying RIP to your fake ID or celebrating your Dirty F*cking Thirty, there is nothing more festive than an ice cream cake! The recipe below is for our most popular cake, Cake Batter Vodka Martini ice cream with layers of funfetti cake. Decorating with rainbow sprinkles and a silly message is optional, but encouraged.

2 boxes Funfetti Cake Mix
1.5 quarts Cake Batter Vodka Martini
Ice Cream (page 52)
16 ounces Frozen Whipped Topping

CAKE INSCRIPTION INSPO

- RIP Fake ID
- Nobody Likes You When You're 23
- You Wanna Piece of Me?
- Finally 21 Bitch
- Cake for One
- You're as Beautiful as This Cake
- Happy 21st Birthday! (+30)
- Let's Get Very Drunk
- Happy Birthday Psycho
- Merry Fucking Christmas
- Happy 14th Birthday!! Wait, I Might be Tipsy...
- #ICECREAMWASTED

Cake Layers:
1. Using your favorite recipe or boxed cake mix, bake three, 9-inch circular layers of cake.
2. Cool in pans 10 minutes and then remove to cool completely.

Ice Cream Layers:
1. Line two 9-inch cake pans with plastic wrap and fill 1-inch high with ice cream.
2. Freeze for at least 8 hours.
1. Place one layer of cake on a cake plate
3. Invert layer of ice cream onto cake layer; remove plastic wrap
4. Add another layer of cake
5. Add second layer of ice cream
6. Add final layer of cake
7. Use a spatula to spread whipped topping over top and sides of cake
8. Freeze for about 2 hours, until firm
9. Optional: Decorate with rainbow sprinkles and a funny inscription!

Congratulations, this year wasn't a complete dumpster fire.

CHAPTER
NINE

PRESENTATION:
TIPS AND TRICKS

BOOZY ICE CREAM FLIGHT

There are whiskey flights, there are beer flights, and then there are boozy ice cream flights! When we opened our first ice cream Barlour we knew we wanted to do a take on the popular "flight" method of sampling spirits. We made it our own with chocolate, sprinkles and a cherry on top!

Plastic Shot Glasses
Melting Chocolate
Rainbow Nonpareils
Assorted Boozy Ice Creams
and Sorbets
Flight Paddle or Serving Tray

PRO TIP: Ice Cream flights look prettier if you use ice creams and sorbets with varying colors! Try Maple Bacon Bourbon (page 24), Mango Margarita (page 36), Chocolate Stout & Salty Pretzel (page 72), and Raspberry Limoncello (page 64)

1. Cover baking sheet with parchment paper.
2. Pour nonpareils into a shallow bowl.
3. Warm melting chocolate in the microwave according to packaging instructions.
4. Dip rim of shot glass about ½ cm deep in melted chocolate and then dip into nonpareils until rim is covered.
5. Place shot glass on parchment lined baking sheet.
6. Repeat for desired number of shot glasses and allow to harden in a cool place for at least 15 minutes.
7. Place shot glasses on flight paddle or tray and use 1oz ice cream scoop to fill with assorted boozy ice creams and sorbets in various colors.
8. Garnish with sprinkles, cherries, and assorted seasonal toppings if desired!

OPEN BAR SUNDAE

Ahhh the Open Bar. Whether it means all the Pinot Grigio you can drink at your cousin's wedding or all the boozy ice cream you can eat in this epic sundae, those are two of our favorite words. This sundae is meant to share! We suggest inviting your friends over this weekend and challenging them to finish the whole "Open Bar." Now that is the ultimate Sundae Funday.

Oversized Martini Glass
Melting Chocolate
Rainbow Nonpareils
Assorted Boozy Ice Creams
and Sorbets
Pocky
Chocolate Olives
Gummy Cherries
Sour Fruit Slices
Edible Glitter
Maraschino Cherries

1. Pour nonpareils into a large bowl.
2. In another large bowl warm melting chocolate in the microwave according to packaging instructions.
3. Dip rim of martini class about ½ inch deep in melted chocolate and then dip into nonpareils until rim is covered.
4. Allow chocolate to harden in a cool place for at least 15 minutes.
5. Scoop 8 large scoops of boozy ice cream and sorbet in assorted flavors into martini glass.
6. Sprinkle sundae with edible glitter.
7. Wedge two Pocky sticks at an angle in one of the top scoops and arrange chocolate olives around sticks.
8. On the other side of the sundae add gummy cherries and sour fruit slices.
9. Top with a maraschino cherry and enjoy with friends

 @feedyourgirlfriend

BOOZY BIRTHDAY SUNDAE

This birthday sundae was created to celebrate the first birthday of our flagship ice cream parlour. It was so popular (and delicious, and beautiful) we brought it back the next year too!

Old Fashioned Ice Cream
Sundae Glass
Cake Batter Vodka Martini
Ice Cream (page 52)
1 box Funfetti Cake Mix
16oz Strawberry Frosting
Rainbow Sprinkles
Maraschino Cherries

> **PRO TIP:** This sundae is on the secret menu at our ice cream balours- you can always order one if it's your birthday!

1. Bake cake in a rectangular sheet pan according to packaging instructions.
2. Allow cake to cool completely and then cut into 1-inch pieces.
3. Fill bottom of sundae glass with layer of rainbow sprinkles .
4. Add layer of cake pieces.
5. Add layer of frosting.
6. Add one large scoop ice cream.
7. Add another layer of sprinkles, cake pieces, and frosting.
8. Top with another large scoop of ice cream.
9. Garnish with more sprinkles, a maraschino cherry, and a colorful candle!

 @newyorkscoops

GROWN UP SUNDAE STATION

Now that you know how to make some of our most popular boozy ice cream treats, it's time to showcase your talents with an ice cream party! A grown up sundae station is the perfect dessert for special occasions like 21st birthdays and engagement parties. For the holidays go all out with pretty seasonal toppings, or add Prosecco to your bar so guests can make their own floats. Boozy ice cream makes every occasion a little more fun—cheers!

Assorted Boozy Ice Creams and Sorbets
Insulated Beverage Tub
Oversized Martini Glass
Oversized Margarita Glass
3 Rocks Glasses or Mason Jars
Small Serving Spoons
Maraschino Cherries
Rainbow Sprinkles
Gummy Bears
Cookie Crumble
Sour Fruit Slices

1. Place beverage tub in the middle of a 4-ft table and fill with ice.
2. Fill oversized martini glass with sprinkles, oversized margarita glass with cherries, and three rocks glasses with other toppings.
3. Insert servings spoons in toppings and arrange on the table around the tub.
4. Fill a quart-sized container with water and two ice cream scoops and place to the left of the beverage tub.
5. On one end of the table put out small bowls, spoons and napkins.
6. As guests arrive remove ice cream pints from the freezer and place in the tub of ice.
7. Invite guests to make their own boozy ice cream sundaes! Our toppings are just suggestions, so swap for your favorites or add even more garnishes to your sundae bar.

INDEX

ACKNOWLEDGEMENTS

Thanks to all of our family and friends for all your love, support, taste testing and heavy lifting over the years. And thanks to the amazing team at Tipsy Scoop for all of your hard work - late nights scooping, potentially hazardous dry ice handling, ice cream cake melting nightmares and more.

To Maddy Chitwood, even though we know you were really afraid to mess up, you certainly did not! Thanks for going above and beyond in designing and editing this book. As usual, we know it was a lot more work than you signed up for!

To Kristin Dickerson and Jessica Maris, the OG managers, for sticking through two summertime store openings, one where we really didn't know what we were doing and one when we sort of did!

To Abby Lavin, for revamping our operations, fixing our fruit fly problem with wine, and generally making our lives a whole lot easier.

To Anthony Gore, for all the packing, deliveries, scary freezer reorganizations, and making sure everything gets done with an "I gotcha, I gotcha" attitude no matter what.

To Danni, John, and the rest of the growing Tipsy Scoop family- thank you for joining the team with immediate enthusiasm and dedication. And for making this year's Christmas party the most lit ever!

To Lyz Levy, for her contribution to this project. From meetings with publishers, to conference calls when she had a new baby, to internal brainstorms to hammer out new structures - thank you so much!

To Ginny Arcari, thank you for the endless arts n' crafts, for inventing the hashtag flags, and for construction projects that probably should have been done by a professional.

To John Tavss, thank you for the free legal aid. We'll be keeping you on retainer.

To Blake Belanger, for all the renovation projects, for all the advice we didn't take, and for helping take care of Riley Bean so we could work on these crazy schemes. And thanks to Riley Belanger, for taste testing our non-alcoholic flavors with your discerning palate.

To Lee Chitwood, thank you for responding to all of our email newsletters - we are glad someone is reading them!

To Pam Chitwood, thank you for being Rachel's constant source of support, love and free therapy. Hope this book makes money so she can start paying you!

To Caroline Jacobs, for all the hard work that first year cracking SO many eggs and lugging the cart around to events all over the city.

To Emily Viviani, for helping Melissa come up with the name, TIPSY SCOOP! And for all the creative support and free labor.

To Security Kyle, for keeping our stores safe and keeping minors away from those boozy scoops.

To Eddie, thanks for transporting us and our ice cream carts all over town! And for never complaining about all the melted ice cream messes, potentially lethal dry ice fumes, and Rachel's constant backseat driving and anxiety about being late!

To Hot Bread Kitchen, for teaching Melissa to always wear a hairnet and how to work and operate in a commercial kitchen.

To Tony and the team at Anthony's Barber shop for always being the kindest neighbors and putting up with our long lines and not always tidy customers.

To Christine Siracusa thank you for the early Saturday morning photo shoots, food styling assistance, and always being willing to try the shot "just one more" way. We couldn't love these photos any more!!!

To all of the influencers who allowed us to use their amazing pictures, thank you!! Especially to Sydelle Anderson the unofficial Tipsy Scoop photographer, party planner, and defender against Instagram hackers.

THANK YOU ALL! We owe you boozy ice cream for life!

PRINTED IN SOUTH KOREA